BROTHER FRANCiS
OF ASSiSi

TOMIE DE PAOLA

BROTHER FRANCIS OF ASSISI

MAGNIFICAT · Ignatius

For Bob Hechtel, Kate Briggs,
and Brother Thomas, O.S.B.

Because of the many different spellings of names encountered in his research, the artist/author has chosen the spellings used by Johannes Jorgensen in his comprehensive biography, *Saint Francis of Assisi*, originally published in 1912 by Longmans, Green & Co., Inc.

The paintings of Francis and Clare were inspired by the fresco of Saint Francis by Cimabue and the fresco of Saint Clare by Simone Martini, both to be found in the lower church of the Basilica of San Francesco in Assisi.

The cross at San Damiano was modeled after the original.

The "Song to the Sun" has been adapted by the artist/author from several translations.

The paintings and initial letters for *Brother Francis of Assisi* were created on 140-pound Fabriano handmade watercolor paper. The artist used transparent inks for the paintings.

VERY FEW CHARACTERS IN HISTORY HAVE CAPTURED THE IMAGINATION AS MUCH AS FRANCIS OF ASSISI AND HIS COMPANION CLARE. They captured mine when I was very young and first heard stories about them. After I graduated from art school, I took a trip to Europe. While in Italy, I traveled to Assisi. It was then and there that I was determined, some day, to recount the tales, in words and paintings, of the two saints. Not an easy task! After all, it meant following such geniuses as Giotto, Cimabue, Simone Martini, Thomas of Celano, G. K. Chesterton, and Nikos Kazantzakis, to mention a few.

As with many "someday projects," much time passed. But in 1978 I returned to Assisi to do photographic research and began to read every account that I could of Francis's and Clare's lives. It was obvious that I could not tell everything about the two saints in an illustrated book. I had to choose which events to include, which to leave out.

So in this book, you, the reader, will not find the story of how Francis visited the Sultan of Egypt or how Clare stopped the Saracens from attacking San Damiano, and many other tales. Instead, I have tried to give you at least a glimpse of their lives; a glimpse into the essential Franciscan spirit—simplicity, joy, the love of nature, and the love of Lady Poverty.

T. de P.

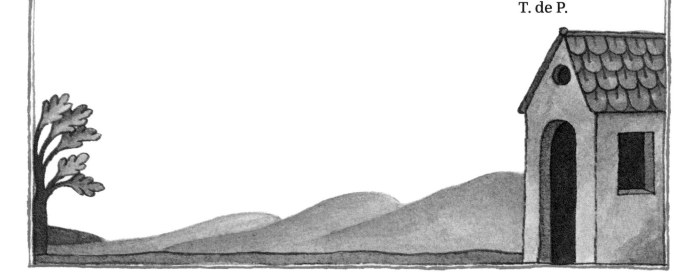

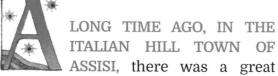 LONG TIME AGO, IN THE ITALIAN HILL TOWN OF ASSISI, there was a great commotion in the house of Don Pietro Di Bernardone, the wealthy cloth merchant.

Don Pietro was away and his young wife, a noblewoman from the south of France, was about to have her first baby.

But the baby would not come. The doctor, the midwife, some lady friends, and all the servants were very worried. Nothing they did seemed to help.

Suddenly there was a knock at the door. An old man dressed as a pilgrim stood there and said, "Tell Donna Pica that she must leave her beautiful bedroom and go to the stable. The child can be born only there."

At once, the doctor, midwife, and friends helped Donna Pica down the stairs, through the house, and across the garden. And there, by the light of a candle, on a fresh bundle of straw, the child was born. It was a boy.

A few days later, the baby was taken to the church of San Rufino and was baptized with the name John.

When Don Pietro returned, he was not pleased with his new son's name.

"Since his mother is French," he declared, "he will be called the 'Frenchman.'"

And so the boy was named Francis.

FRANCIS WAS ALWAYS IN TROUBLE. Wearing flashy clothes, he rushed around Assisi with his friends, eating, drinking, and having a good time.

Many a night, the good people of Assisi were awakened from a sound sleep by the noise of loud singing and guitar music.

Looking out their windows, they would catch a glimpse of a hat with a long red feather.

"Ah," they would say, "it is Francis again. Does he never sleep?"

One day, Francis was pushing through the noisy crowds in the narrow streets.

All around him, the people were talking about war against the neighboring city of Perugia.

Suddenly a beggar stopped him. The beggar took off his tattered cloak and threw it on the ground, as if Francis were a prince and the cloak was a carpet for him to walk on.

"I have no coins," Francis said.

"I don't want any!" said the beggar. "I do this to honor you, for soon you will do great things that will be talked about until the end of the world."

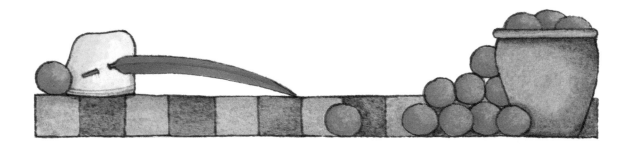

FRANCIS DI BERNARDONE WAS NOT HAPPY. Something was wrong. He had joined the battle against Perugia and had been captured and held prisoner for a year.

Returning to Assisi, he had fallen gravely ill and had not been able to leave his bed for many months.

When news of another great war had reached Assisi, Don Pietro had outfitted Francis in a splendid suit of armor. He had given Francis a powerful horse, so he could go and become a knight.

But Francis had given his armor and horse away. He had fallen ill again and returned home. Everything had changed.

More and more, Francis spent time in the fields around Assisi. He began to pray a great deal. He even did something that he never would have done before. He kissed the fingers of a leper.

Donna Pica was very worried about her son, but Don Pietro was angry. As far as he was concerned, Francis had gone mad!

Francis started to go to the little church of San Damiano to pray before the old painted cross. Even though the church was in a bad state of disrepair, he felt a great deal of peace there.

One day Francis entered San Damiano and began to pray as usual. "Lord," he prayed, "what do you want of me?"

And the crucifix spoke.

"Francis," the Lord said, "rebuild my church. It is falling down."

The old priest in charge of the church was outside on a stone bench, sunning himself, when Francis came rushing out. Francis thrust a bag of coins into his hands.

"This money is to buy oil for the altar lamp. Let me know when you need more. I am going to rebuild the church."

Before the old priest could recover from his surprise, Francis was gone.

And the life of Francis would never be the same.

DON PIETRO DI BERNARDONE wanted to disown his son Francis. First of all, Francis had stolen bolts of cloth and a horse and sold them. He had given the money to the old priest at San Damiano. It was lucky for Don Pietro that the priest was afraid of the large sum and had returned it. Then Francis had disappeared for a month and had come home dirty, looking like a beggar. The boys had chased him and called him "un pazzo"—a crazy man. Francis had become a fool! Don Pietro had no other choice but to lock him up. However, as soon as Don Pietro had left on a trip, Donna Pica had released Francis. He had flown like a bird back to San Damiano. His mother had also given him more money. Don Pietro wanted that money back. The law had refused the case. So the only thing left to do was to bring Francis before the bishop.

Inside the bishop's palace, everyone listened as Don Pietro di Bernardone angrily listed his complaints. Francis sat quietly. Finally the bishop said to Francis, "My son, what do you wish?"

"To serve God, my Lord," answered Francis.

"If indeed you wish to serve God," the bishop said, "return the money to your father. God does not want his work advanced with money unjustly gained."

Francis stood. "My Lord," he said, "I will cheerfully give my father not only the money, but everything else he has given me!"

At that, Francis stepped behind a tapestry hanging on the wall. A moment later, he reappeared. He was naked. He laid the clothes and money at his father's feet.

"Until now I have called Pietro di Bernardone father. I am returning his money and all the clothes he has given to me. From now on, I shall not say 'Father Pietro di Bernardone,' but 'Our Father who is in heaven!'"

The crowd cheered, "Bravo! Bravo for Francis!" The bishop stepped forward and covered Francis with his cloak. Don Pietro, filled with rage, picked up the clothes and money and left.

Then the bishop gave Francis an old robe that had belonged to a gardener. Francis drew a cross on the back of it with a piece of chalk. He left the bishop's palace on that sunny April day to go out into the world.

Francis had never felt happier.

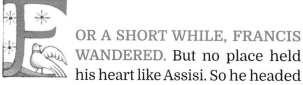OR A SHORT WHILE, FRANCIS WANDERED. But no place held his heart like Assisi. So he headed back to the town of his birth. After all, there was still the church of San Damiano to rebuild. But how would he buy stones and mortar and tools? What could he do? He knew how to sing. He would sing for stones.

So, in the marketplace of Assisi, Francis sang like a wandering minstrel. And when he had finished his songs, he begged. "He who gives me a stone will be rewarded in heaven," he cried. "If you give me two stones, you will have two rewards; three stones, three rewards."

Some laughed at Francis, but many were moved by the change the love of God had made in him. People began to give him stones. And mortar, too. He carried them on his back down to San Damiano. And with borrowed tools, he began to rebuild the church with his own hands, just as the Lord had told him to do.

Before long, the church of San Damiano stood repaired. But Francis did not stop. He repaired the old church of San Pietro. And finally, the little field chapel of Santa Maria degli Angeli or, as it was called, Portiuncula.

One morning during Mass at Portiuncula, Francis heard these words of Jesus from the Gospel: "Take no gold, nor silver, nor copper in your belts, no bag for your journey, nor two tunics, nor sandals, nor a staff; for the laborer deserves his food."

Francis took off his shoes and threw away his walking stick and the cloak he wore to keep warm. He threw away his belt and tied a piece of rope around his rough robe. Full of joy, he went up to Assisi and sang about the wonderful love of God. He was so happy that he began to dance. And he danced and danced.

This time the people did not laugh at Francis; they were filled with his joy, too. "Is he a crazy man?" someone asked.

"I am God's fool!" Francis answered.

"It is Francis, the son of di Bernardone," someone said.

"I am Francis, the poor man of Assisi," said Francis.

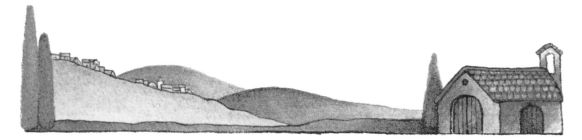

T WAS NOT LONG BEFORE WORD OF FRANCIS, the Poor Man of Assisi, reached many ears—the little man who danced and sang with the joy of God, the little man who owned nothing, who greeted everyone with the words, "The Lord give you peace."

And it was not long before other men came to Francis to live as he did.

The first two, Bernardo di Quintavalle and Pietro dei Cattani, went with Francis to the church of San Niccolo, where they prayed together. Then Francis went to the Gospel on the altar. He opened it and read, "If you would be perfect, go, sell what you possess and give to the poor, and you will have treasure in heaven."

Again, Francis opened the book. He read, "If any man would come after me, let him deny himself and take up his cross and follow me." And a third time, Francis read, "He charged them to take nothing for their journey."

"My brothers, these words of Jesus will be our life and our Rule," said Francis. "Not only for us but for anyone else who wishes to live with us. Now, go and do what you have heard."

Bernardo and Pietro gave away all their possessions and put on robes with rope belts. Francis led them down to Portiuncula, where they made a hut of branches plastered with mud. There they slept at night and prayed during the day. They called each other brother and begged for their food, telling everyone they met about the joy of God.

Soon there were more brothers. The tiny hut was too small for so many, so they moved to a shed in a place called Rivo Torto.

Winter was cold, and sometimes the brothers would have nothing to eat. They were all hungry. But Brother Francis would start to sing and dance with the joy of God, and the hunger would vanish.

NE DAY, BROTHER FRANCIS CALLED ALL THE BROTHERS TOGETHER. "There are now twelve of us. We must go to Rome to receive the pope's blessing for our way of life."

Amid the splendor of the bishops, the cardinals, and the pope himself, Francis and his brothers looked small and poor indeed.

Brother Francis was asked to read his Rule. In a clear voice, Francis read, "We are to be called the least of all brothers. Let no brother own anything. Let the brothers beg for their food. Let the brothers live in complete poverty."

Silence filled the huge room. Then Pope Innocent III spoke. "My dear son, your Rule seems too severe to me. I do not doubt that *you* are able to live it, but think of those who will come after you. They may not have the same strength and courage."

"Holy Father," Francis said, "we depend upon the Lord. Surely he will not deny us what we need on earth to live."

"What you say is true," the pope replied. "But man is frail. Go and pray that is what God wants of you."

A few days later, Francis and the brothers were called back.

The Holy Father told them about a dream. In the dream, he had seen the Lateran church begin to topple. Suddenly a little man appeared. He was dressed in a rough robe with a rope around his waist instead of a belt. The man leaned against the crumbling walls. With a mighty push, the man straightened the church. It was saved. The little man turned, and the pope saw that it was Francis.

It was decided! Pope Innocent III embraced Brother Francis and blessed him and the brothers. "Go with God," the pope said. "You have my blessing for your Rule. May you become many."

It was with great happiness that the brothers left for Assisi. They sang and danced all the way home.

And Francis sang that, truly, Lady Poverty had become his bride.

HEN FRANCIS AND THE BROTHERS RETURNED TO ASSISI, more followers wanted to join them. The shed at Rivo Torto was becoming far too small. Francis had always loved the little chapel of Portiuncula. It would be the perfect place for all of them to live.

It was a joyful day when the monks on Monte Subasio, who owned the chapel, gave the brotherhood the privilege of using Portiuncula forever.

Francis reminded the brothers that the Rule forbade them to own anything. Instead, they would send a basket of fish to the monks each year as payment of rent.

At the side of the chapel, Francis and the brothers built huts. A tall hedge made perfect walls for the little convent. The bare earth was both table and chairs, and the brothers slept on sacks of straw.

Every day, it seemed that new brothers came. And every day brothers went out to preach the joy of God.

"Let us not forget," Brother Francis said, "that we are not only brothers, but we are the *littlest* brothers, the least of all. We shall be called Friars Minor."

And so the new brotherhood finally had a name.

SSISI WAS FILLED WITH EXCITEMENT. Brother Francis had returned and was to preach at San Rufino.

Among the people who heard him that day was a daughter of the wealthy Scifi family. Her name was Clare.

From the first moment she heard Francis speak, Clare decided that the life he led was to be hers as well.

Secretly, through the winter, Clare and Brother Francis met. They spoke of God and joy and holy poverty.

On the night of Palm Sunday, Clare dressed in her finest clothes and left her father's house. With her old aunt Bona Guelfucci at her side, Clare went into the dark woods, where torches could be seen in the distance. The brothers were coming to meet her.

Francis was waiting at Portiun‐cula. Clare exchanged her shining silk gown for a rough, woolen robe, just as the brothers wore. She gave up her jeweled belt for a piece of knotted rope. Taking off her embroidered slippers, she put wooden sandals on her bare feet. Then, letting her golden hair loose, Clare bowed her head as Francis picked up the shears that had been placed on the altar. Three or four swift cuts, and the hair lay on the ground around her. Clare then put on the veil of a nun. She vowed holy poverty, and she promised to obey Brother Francis as her superior.

That same night, Francis took her to the Benedictine Sisters at the convent of San Paolo, where she would stay for a short time.

Clare's father, Favorino Scifi, was known for his violent temper. When he heard what had happened, he gathered his male relatives and went to the convent to get Clare back. As they tried to drag Clare away by force, she clung to the altar, and pulling off the black veil, she showed her cropped hair. There was nothing more to do.

Lady Clare Scifi had become Sister Clare.

SIXTEEN DAYS AFTER CLARE HAD EMBRACED LADY POVERTY, Agnes, Clare's younger sister, also left home and came to the convent of Sant'Angelo, where Clare was now staying. She too wished to live as a follower of Francis.

Favorino Scifi was even more furious. What madness had taken hold of his daughters? In a wild rage, he ordered his brother Monaldo to take twelve armed men and bring Agnes home.

The nuns at Sant'Angelo were terrified at the sight of the weapons and left poor Agnes to face the men by herself.

The men used force and dragged Agnes from the convent.

"Clare! Clare! Come help me," Agnes cried.

Clare prayed to God for help.

Suddenly the twelve stout men could not move Agnes one inch further. She became as heavy as lead. Monaldo was so furious that he lifted his armored fist to crush the girl's head with one blow. But again a miracle occurred. Monaldo stood frozen, his arm upraised but unable to move.

The men knew they could not win. The family made no more attempts to make the young women return.

Clare and Agnes and a few others who joined them were given the little convent next to San Damiano. The Poor Sisters, as they were called, lived the same life as the brothers. Some worked at home, others went out and begged. But above all, they lived a life of poverty.

Soon Clare and Agnes were joined by their youngest sister, Beatrice. And after their father's death, their mother, Ortolana, also joined them.

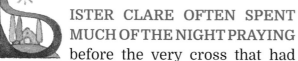ISTER CLARE OFTEN SPENT MUCH OF THE NIGHT PRAYING before the very cross that had spoken to Brother Francis. Even so, she was always the first one up in the morning, ringing the bell for Mass and lighting the lamps. Although she held the position of abbess, she served the other sisters, nursing them when they were ill and waiting on table. When the sisters came home from begging, Clare would wash their feet.

One feast day, the pope came to San Damiano for a visit and to share a meal with the Poor Sisters.

"Holy Father," said Clare, "will you be so kind as to bless the bread?"

"Ah, Sister Clare," the pope replied, "indeed, I ask *you* to bless the bread," for he was very moved by Clare's holiness.

Because the pope insisted, Sister Clare made the Sign of the Cross over the loaves.

Suddenly on every loaf a cross appeared.

The pope knew that he had just seen a miracle.

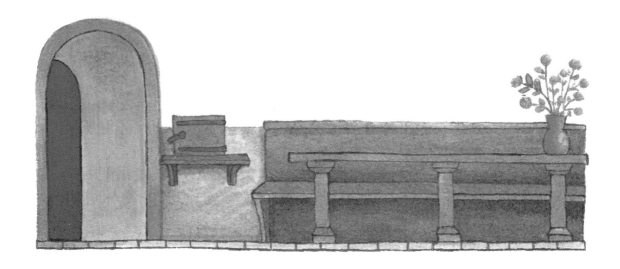

ROTHER FRANCIS BEGAN TO THINK OF RETIRING FROM THE WORLD and becoming a hermit. But the Lord told him, through Sister Clare and some of the brothers, that he should go out and preach. So taking along Brother Masseo and Brother Angelo, he set out immediately.

On the way, Brother Francis saw some trees by the roadside filled with birds of all kinds. And a great many were also on the ground.

"Wait here for me!" Francis said. "I am going to preach to my sisters."

"Sister birds," he said as the birds gathered around him, "you owe God much thanks and ought always and everywhere to praise him. He has given you the joy to fly freely. The whole sky is yours. He has given you warm feathers like thick cloaks. You do not have to sew or spin for your living. God feeds you and gives you water to drink from the rivers and streams. He gives you tall trees to nest in, mountains and valleys for shelter. Each of you has a song. Do you see how God loves you? So, watch that you are never ungrateful. Stay simple and poor as an example to people. And praise and thank our Father every day. Your song is your prayer. So, sing, my sisters. Praise him."

Brother Francis blessed the birds. The birds rose up and began to fly away. The sound of their singing filled the sky.

I N THE TOWN OF GUBBIO, THERE WAS A LARGE AND TERRIFYING WOLF who ate men as well as animals. All the townspeople were so afraid that they dared not go out.

Brother Francis decided he would try to help. He went down the path that led to the wolf's lair. The wolf rushed out to meet Francis, its teeth glaring in the sun. Making the Sign of the Cross in the air, Francis called, "Come here, Brother Wolf, in the name of the Lord."

Hearing these words, the wolf closed its mouth and lay down like a lamb at the feet of Francis.

Francis talked to the wolf, scolding it for being so fierce. "You must promise to stop this killing, and I shall ask the people of Gubbio to feed you until the end of your days. Do you agree?" The wolf bowed its head in agreement. So, Brother Francis brought the wolf into the town square. The people were frightened, but Francis raised his hand to calm them.

"Good people," Francis said, "Brother Wolf promises to stop all his killing if you will promise to feed him daily until the end of his life. Do you agree?"

With one voice the people agreed.

"And you, Brother Wolf, give me a sign that you too will observe the peace in the name of the Lord."

The wolf bowed its head, and then lifted up a paw and placed it in Francis's hand.

For two years, Brother Wolf went from house to house, door to door, and was fed by the good people of Gubbio. The wolf in turn did no more harm.

After two years, Brother Wolf died of old age. And the people missed him.

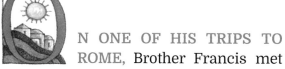N ONE OF HIS TRIPS TO ROME, Brother Francis met one of his most faithful followers. Her name was Jacopa de Settesoli. Although she came from wealth and had married into wealth, she lived a life of simplicity and poverty.

When Brother Francis was taken to meet her, he expected to find a house filled with riches. But not so. Jacopa showed Francis her room. It was like a room of a monk—white stone walls, a plain wooden table, two chairs, and a sack filled with straw for a bed. The only thing on the wall was a simple cross.

Instead of a rich meal and strong wine, she offered Francis plain bread and water.

"Because you are like a true brother of mine," Francis said, "I shall call you Brother Jacopa."

Whenever he visited her, Francis could live in poverty as he did at Portiuncula. However, Brother Francis let Brother Jacopa spoil him in one small way.

She baked fine cakes for her children. They were made of honey, ground almonds, and wheat flour.

"You must taste these cakes," Brother Jacopa said. Francis ate one. He ate three, five, seven...

"I shall never forget this taste," said Francis. Then he, who never seemed to care about what he ate, gobbled down more of the wonderful cakes without any shame.

BROTHER FRANCIS, SO FILLED WITH THE LOVE OF GOD, began to greet all of God's creatures whenever he met them.

He would greet Sister Fire, Brother Sun, Sister Moon, Sister Water, Brother Tree...

Francis felt kinship with everything on the earth. He especially had a great love for Brother Lamb.

He could never stand to see one of the creatures being led to slaughter, and he would try everything to save it.

Once he convinced a merchant to give him a lamb he was selling, and since Brother Francis was on his way to see the bishop, the lamb came along with him.

On another occasion, Francis gave his cloak in exchange for two small lambs that a peasant was taking to the butcher.

There was a tame lamb at Portiuncula, which followed Brother Francis everywhere. And one time when Francis was in Rome, he saved a lamb he then gave to Brother Jacopa. This lamb lived a very long time in Brother Jacopa's house. It followed her to Mass every morning. It was so eager to go to church that it would butt its head against its mistress to wake her if she was late in getting up. Brother Jacopa spun its wool and wove it into fine woolen cloth. Some day, she would make a new robe for Brother Francis.

ONE CHRISTMAS EVE, Francis and some brothers were staying near Greccio on a wooded cliff high above the town. It had been given to them by their friend Giovanni Vellita. Francis said to him:

"I want to celebrate the Holy Christmas Mass with you in a special way this year. There is a cave in the woods by the cloister. Bring a manger to the cave and fill the manger with hay. Also, we will need an ox and an ass just as in Bethlehem on the night the Lord was born. For once, I want to celebrate the coming of the Lord seriously, so we may see how poor and humble he wished to be for our sakes."

Giovanni did as Francis asked, and as midnight of Christmas Eve approached, all the brothers came with torches and candles to celebrate. The little cave was dazzling with light. The Mass was said over the manger as an altar.

And then it seemed to Giovanni that he saw a real child lying in the manger. Brother Francis came forward and took the child lovingly in his arms. The child smiled at Francis and stroked his beard and coarse robe.

The celebration ended, and all who were there went home with joy. They had truly celebrated the birth of the Holy King.

SISTER CLARE HAD NOT SEEN BROTHER FRANCIS FOR A LONG WHILE. She sent word to Francis that she would like the honor of having a meal with him and the brothers at Portiuncula. Six times she asked and six times Francis said no. Sister Clare treated him like a saint, and that he did not like.

The other brothers thought it a pity. "It was because of you that Sister Clare took up the life of poverty. It would give her such happiness," they pleaded. Francis finally agreed to see her.

The morning arrived, and some brothers went to get Sister Clare. Now that Sister Clare was coming, Francis was glad. Now he could greet *her* as a saint.

Francis bowed to Sister Clare and kissed her robe. He took her hand which had grown dark and rough from hard work and led her into the little church where years before Francis had cut her hair.

Then they went to the guest house, where a feast had been spread on the bare ground. There was cheese, bread, and milk. Clare and the sister who had come with her sat, and all the brothers sat, too.

Broth was poured into wooden bowls, and Brother Francis said grace.

Suddenly, because of Clare's pure soul, Brother Francis began to speak so fervently of God that everyone there became inflamed with his love.

Up on a hill, some shepherds looked and saw a blaze in the sky.

"Look, Portiuncula and the Little Brothers' huts are all on fire," they said.

Later they found out it was just the blaze of the holy souls of Brother Francis and Sister Clare speaking of the Lord.

BROTHER FRANCIS WAS NOT WELL. He could barely see. His eyes burned from a sickness in them that began when he went to preach in the Holy Land. His poor body was thin and sore from fasting and the life of holy poverty. But still Francis went with some brothers to the wild mountain of Alverna. It was a favorite place of his, because there he could be alone.

Brother Francis told the brothers that he wished to see no one. Brother Leo might bring some water from time to time, but nobody else was to come near him.

Francis went to a cave on the other side of a deep chasm. He told Brother Leo to leave bread at the end of the plank bridge and to call out. If Francis answered, then Brother Leo was to come and pray with him; but if there was no answer, Brother Leo was to go away.

On the Feast of the Holy Cross, Francis, the Poor Man of Assisi, was praying outside the cave. It was near dawn. The stars filled the sky.

All of a sudden there was a dazzling light. There, in the light, was a fiery figure with six wings nailed to a cross of fire. The wounds in the hands and feet and side glowed like jewels. The face was the face of the Lord, and the Lord spoke.

Then streams of light shot from the wounds of the Lord and pierced the hands and feet and side of Francis. With a great cry of love, Brother Francis sank to the ground. He now carried the wounds of the Lord himself.

ROTHER FRANCIS LAY DYING. The Brothers made him as comfortable as possible in the little hut at Portiuncula. He was blind. The wounds in his hands and feet and side burned and blazed. There was scarcely any flesh on his body. But still Brother Francis sang with the joy of God. Brother Jacopa came to see him, bringing his favorite cakes and a fine woolen robe she had woven from the wool of the lamb Brother Francis had saved years before.

One by one the brothers came for his blessings. The Little Brothers— the Friars Minor— were all over the world now. The Poor Sisters had many members, too.

The brothers gathered. "Sing my brothers," Francis said. "Sing the *Song to the Sun.*" It was a song Brother Francis had written when he could no longer see.

The singing filled the air around Portiuncula.

"Sing it again, my brothers, and this time," Francis said, "let us sing the welcome to Sister Death."

BROTHER FRANCIS WELCOMED SISTER DEATH as the sun set. Both Francis and the birds were singing when Sister Death came.

The brothers dressed Brother Francis in the robe Brother Jacopa had brought.

The next morning, word of Brother Francis's death reached the people of Assisi. They came with candles and olive branches.

Then, in procession, they carried his body to San Damiano, so Clare and her sisters could bid their brother farewell. The procession passed through Assisi to the church of San Giorgio. There, the people said goodbye to Francis, their brother, their saint—the Poor Man of Assisi.

THE SONG TO THE SUN

Most High, Almighty and All-good Lord!
   All blessings, praise, all glory and honor
      are Yours!

Only to You, Most High, do they belong,
   And no one is worthy to say Your Name.

Be praised, my Lord, through all Your creatures!
   Sir Brother Sun is the first.
   With him, You give us light of day.

For he is beautiful and radiant, he is full of splendor;
   He is the symbol of You, Most High!

Be praised, my Lord, for Sister Moon and all the Stars!
   You placed them in the sky;
   And made them bright and lovely and fair.

Be praised, my Lord, for Brother Wind
    and Brother Air,
   Cloudy, clear, and all weather;
   By which You nourish all creatures.

Be praised, my Lord, for Sister Water!
    How useful she is, how humble;
    She is precious and chaste!

Be praised, my Lord, for Brother Fire,
    For him, You make bright the dark!
    He is beautiful, he is merry;
    He is powerful and strong!

Be praised, my Lord, for Sister Earth!
    She is the mother who governs us and gives us food.
    For us, she makes all kinds of fruits;
    All colors of flowers, and sweet herbs.

Be praised, my Lord, for those who forgive
    because they love You;
    For those who bear sickness and trials.

They are happy, who accept all in peace,
    For they will be crowned by You, Most High!

Be praised, my Lord, for Sister Death!
    No mortal can escape her kiss.

Woeful are those who die in mortal sin.

But happy are those who do Your will,
    For the Second Death will not harm them.

Praise and bless my Lord; thank Him.
    And serve Him with great humility.

IT IS IN VISITING ASSISI THAT ONE REALLY GETS TO KNOW FRANCIS AND CLARE. Their spirits still pervade the Umbrian hill town which has changed little since the two saints lived there. It is not hard to imagine the young Francis rushing through the still, narrow streets among the buildings of pink-gold stone and soft-red tiled roofs.

At **San Damiano**, you can see clearly how Clare and her sisters lived. In the refectory, Clare's place is marked by a simple copper vase always filled with flowers.

In the **Basilica of Santa Chiara**, the pre-Gothic cross, the cross that legend says spoke to Francis, hangs in a side chapel. It is very beautiful.

But the most touching sight of all is the **tomb of Saint Francis** in the crypt of the Basilica of San Francesco. It is a simple, rough stone sarcophagus, bound with iron bands, as simple and humble as the life of the saint himself. Hundreds of candles burn before it, and hundreds of pieces of paper with petitions written on them lie around it. It is here one really meets Francis, the Poor Man of Assisi.

T. de P.

1182 Birth of Saint Francis
1194 Birth of Saint Clare
1206 The cross speaks to Francis at San Damiano.
1209 Pope Innocent III gives oral approval of the Rule.
1212 Clare receives the habit.
1224 Francis receives the stigmata at Alverna.
1226 Francis dies on October 4 at Portiuncula.
1228 Francis is proclaimed a saint.
1230 The body of Saint Francis is taken to the Basilica of San Francesco, on May 25.
1253 Clare dies at San Damiano.
1255 Clare is proclaimed a saint.
1818 The body of Saint Francis is rediscovered, after 600 years,
during excavations in the basilica.
1928 Pope Pius XII proclaims Francis Patron of Italy.

The **Feast day of Saint Clare** is August 12.
The **Feast day of Saint Francis** is October 4.
Pope John Paul II proclaimed **Francis Patron of Ecology** on November 29, 1979.

Under the direction of **Romain Lizé**, CEO, MAGNIFICAT
Editor, MAGNIFICAT: **Isabelle Galmiche**
Editor, Ignatius: **Vivian Dudro**
Proofreader: **Kathleen Hollenbeck**
Assistant to the Editor: **Pascale van de Walle**
Layout Designer: **Jean-Marc Richard**
Production: **Thierry Dubus, Sabine Marion**i

First published by Holiday House, New York, NY: © 1982 by Tomie dePaola

Second edition: @ 2020 by MAGNIFICAT, New York • Ignatius Press, San Francisco
All rights reserved.
ISBN Ignatius Press 978-1-62164-369-2 • ISBN MAGNIFICAT 978-1-949239-26-3

Printed in July 2021 by DZS, in Ljubljana, Slovenia.
Job number MGN 21038-02.
Printed in compliance with the Consumer Protection Safety Act, 2008